D1062534

For my very special Dad

With love from

Other books in this series:
Best Friends
Thank you Mum
I've got a crush on you
Have a Perfect Day
Stay Calm

Published in 2010 by Helen Exley Giftbooks in Great Britain. A copy of the CIP data is available from the British Library on request. All rights reserved. No part of this publication may be reproduced or transmitted in any form or by any means, electronic or mechanical, including photocopy, recording or any information storage and retrieval system without permission in writing from the Publisher.
Printed in China.

Words and illustrations © Jenny Kempe 2010
Design and arrangement © Exley Publications 2010
The moral right of the author has been asserted.

12 11 10 9 8 7 6 5 4 3 2

ISBN: 978-1-84634-491-6

Dedication: To Lars, my super dad.

Published by HELEN EXLEY®
Helen Exley Giftbooks, 16 Chalk Hill, Watford, Herts WD19 4BG, UK.
www.helenexleygiftbooks.com

My Dad, My Hero

WORDS AND ILLUSTRATIONS BY

JENNY KEMPE

Thank you for
doing the same trick
over and over
– and over and over
– and over and over
again.

Thank you for coming home
with nice surprises.

Thank you

for being my biggest fan.

Dad, for arranging trips
to do super-special things.

Thank you.

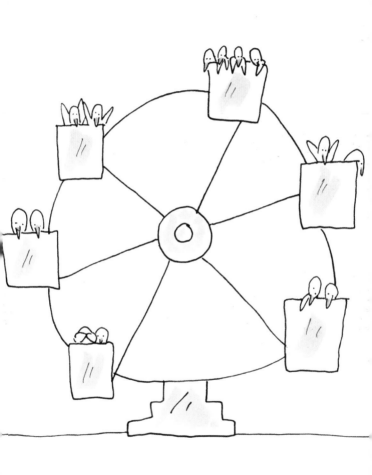

Thank you for helping me

master new skills.

Thank you for helping me

to be brave.

Thank you, Dad.
You have always
believed in me.

Thank you for our time together

– just you and me.

Dad, thank you
for telling me
about distant places.
For inspiring me.
For making me dream.

Thank you for taking
my friend and me
on big adventures.

Thank you for teaching
me about the world.
Strange things. Funny things.
Dangerous things.

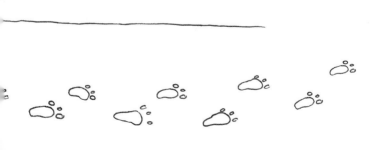

Thank you for protecting me.

Dad, for reading to me,
for helping me
with all my work;
For our quiet times together.
Thank you.

Thank you for saying
that to do one's best,
is all that counts.

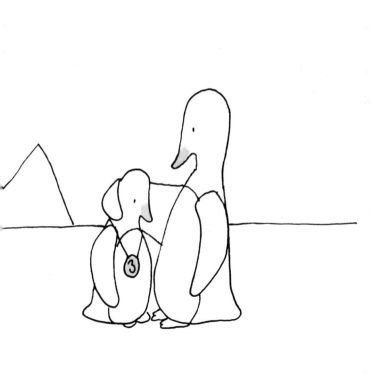

For all the cuddles,
for all the help and support,
for being MY dad:
Thank you.

You're my hero.

And I love you loads.

Jenny Kempe

In 2009, overwhelmed by the endless bad news in the media, Jenny Kempe decided to take a six month break from newspapers, TV and radio. She turned her focus to the things in life that made her happy; to friends and family and to "taking time to just be". The result is the wonderfully bright and positive gift book series "Life is Beautiful". Each title has been designed to warm your heart and to put a smile on your face. As gifts, these books will brighten up the day, or even the life, of someone you care for.

About Helen Exley gifts

Helen Exley products cover the most powerful range of all human relationships: love between couples, the bonds within families and between friends. No expense is spared in making sure that each book is as thoughtful and meaningful a gift as it is possible to create: good to give, good to receive. You have the result in your hands. If you have loved it – tell others!

Visit our website to see all of Helen Exley's other books and gifts: **www.helenexleygiftbooks.com**

Helen Exley Giftbooks
16 Chalk Hill, Watford, Herts
WD19 4BG, UK
www.helenexleygiftbooks.com

We loved making this book for you.
We hope you'll enjoy the other titles
in our series Life is Beautiful.

The Life is Beautiful Team